Praise for *I Say the Sky*

"*I Say the Sky* distills ordinary passing moments of a world made striking, made memorable. But as the poet disperses such moments into the poems, that world is made strange, made unsayable. Whatever has been named vanishes into something else; whatever has been exiled returns on the next horizon: next line, next verse, next poem. In Colburn's poetics, a pinpoint of memory foreshadows an unshakable sense of dislocation, the strangeness of inhabiting a body and a world in which we can never be just one thing. All the while the ineffable, even the unbearable, runs to meet joy. . . . Certain load-bearing words—stones, hands, a voice, the sky, to name a few—orchestrate a controlled music that surprises us and sends us back to read them again and again. What more could one ask of poetry?"

—Annie G. Rogers,
professor of psychology and author of
The Unsayable: The Hidden Language of Trauma

"Colburn connects words to earth, body to family, and family to nature. Here, language is sacred; uttering a word, composing a line, writing a stanza is a prayer of joy, even if the context is loss. Even loss can be an occasion to be grateful. Colburn has given poetry a breath that revives it, that urges others to see deeper and reclaim their humanity."

—Jimmy Santiago Baca,
author of *A Place to Stand*

"*I Say the Sky* is made of timely and urgent questions. 'What is missing? In the house of my life.' With skillful metacognition, Colburn approaches the inexpressible and explores ephemerality, trauma, ecological devastation, and how everything connects to the quotidian. These poems are wonderfully awake to our unspeakable lives. She writes: 'I want so badly to live sometimes I forget / that I am alive.' In this collection Colburn couples gravity with gratitude and creates a bright infusion of healing and regeneration."

—Laynie Browne,
author of *Translation of the Lilies Back into Lists*

"In *I Say the Sky*, the poet sees our world with its obvious need of repair and our inability to agree on the name of that repair. In that space she goes after the crystalline beauty of delivering the lyric from inside the human heart as it presses its rhythm against the rhythm of our world, naming the precious things only a poet who values the present moment can know. What a wonderful collection Colburn has wrought."

—Afaa M. Weaver,
Kingsley Tufts Poetry Award winner and author of *A Fire in the Hills*

"Nadia Colburn has written a marvelous book of poetry that will appeal to poetry lovers everywhere. These poems speak to the human condition and its transitions and transformations, making meaning of life's difficulties and showing us how to turn them into celebrations. I recommend their imagery, beauty, and powerful metaphors to everyone."

—Lewis Mehl-Madrona, MD,
author of *Coyote Medicine*

"The tender, fierce poems that populate *I Say Sky* are poems that vow to be present: 'This is not a poem about escape / The great transition is not an escape / but a turn in which we meet the self / we may not want to meet.' These great transitions are momentous—birth and death—but they also exist in hours of quotidian caregiving that hum with meaning. Cutting carrots, reading a book aloud to a child, planting seeds, and even sitting in silent stillness demand the body's attention. The permeable, powerful female body, the (un)sung hero of this book, knows the generosity of speech, of gesture, of touch, of saying in all its bodily forms. In an act of communion with the world, *I Say Sky* seeks to 'translate the spruce forest of [the] heart' for all whose ears are open to hear."

—Sasha Steensen,
author of *Everything Awake*

I
SAY
THE SKY

I
SAY
THE SKY

POEMS

NADIA COLBURN

UNIVERSITY PRESS OF KENTUCKY

Scholarly publisher for the Commonwealth, serving Bellarmine University, Berea College, Centre College of Kentucky, Eastern Kentucky University, The Filson Historical Society, Georgetown College, Kentucky Historical Society, Kentucky State University, Morehead State University, Murray State University, Northern Kentucky University, Spalding University, Transylvania University, University of Kentucky, University of Louisville, University of Pikeville, and Western Kentucky University.
All rights reserved.

Editorial and Sales Offices: The University Press of Kentucky
663 South Limestone Street, Lexington, Kentucky 40508-4008
www.kentuckypress.com

Cataloging-in-Publication data available from the Library of Congress

ISBN 978-0-8131-9863-7 (hardcover)
ISBN 978-0-8131-9864-4 (paperback)
ISBN 978-0-8131-9866-8 (pdf)
ISBN 978-0-8131-9865-1 (epub)

This book is printed on acid-free paper meeting the requirements of the American National Standard for Permanence in Paper for Printed Library Materials.

Manufactured in the United States of America.

Member of the Association
of University Presses

*For Eric, Gabriel, and Simone
with love beyond language*

i am accused of tending to the past as if i made it,
as if i sculpted it
with my own hands.
—*LUCILLE CLIFTON*

There was never any more inception than there is now,
Nor any more youth or age than there is now,
And will never be any more perfection than there is now,
Nor any more heaven or hell than there is now.
—*WALT WHITMAN*

Contents

I Think It Is Such a Beautiful

dawn
          and my mind,
which wants to hold things
as they are, cannot hold
this morning,
       first of April,   spring too early
this year by three weeks,
              the daffodils
of my city spurred forward
by the warmth—

cannot hold Brett,
              gone,
Patrizia, gone—

      not the marching clouds,
      not the sky that is perched, unaltering,
              above the clouds,
      not the methane leaks,
      not the whales
           suffering the piercing
sounds of boats:

I reach out my hands: one
and then the other,
          spread my fingers as light

falls through them.

Upflying

Whole flocks of geese in my childhood honking their way
North—

The streets dirty with pigeons—

The sky blackened by starlings, each small, pointed wing
so close to another's it was just a blur—

Now, three billion birds are missing.

We wake to so many forms of emptiness;
so much loss greets us in our sleep.

In my childhood, I thought the world I'd entered
would be the one I'd exit.

In the poplar, one grackle whistles,
not to me.

Smaller Even than Last Week
(for Ruth)

She sits in her wheelchair, huddled
over the oxygen that is pumped
through a paper cup
up in the direction of her nose
as she struggles for breath, ready or not
for the great transition.

Her son greets us with jokes, asks about our
New Year's resolutions, about whether we saw
the new store on the road before
we turned off to the nursing home.

She opens her eyes, grunts, tells him
to stop.

This is important work.

We get up, put Mozart's flute concerto
on the old boom box and do not
talk.

I don't know if this is the proper
material for a poem, the almost
death of an old lady I have come to almost
love.

Why not? Why hesitate? And why call
what I feel for her almost
love? What stone within my heart
prevents me from giving myself
completely?

At night, when we are home, I think
of her beautiful face, her eyelids always elegant,
her smile at my daughter the same
as it has always been.

I think of her desire to protect the young—
her mother dying
when she was ten, and the Nazis
soon to take over Hannover,
she and her sister surviving
only because they were twins—
protection, what she did not
get, what she could not entirely give
her own children, the suffering
seeping out.

This is not a poem about escape.
The great transition is not an escape
but a turn in which we meet the self
we may not want to meet.

And then what happens?

Last year, at almost the same time, our friend's heart stopped
for a moment. Two months later she saw
shadows, *they are coming,* she said,
terrified, fighting against them with all her force
as I sat on her bed—the dark
approaching, but nothing, not even her own
ten-year-old twins, could keep her fastened
to this life.

Darling. Forgive me.

Forgive me for what?
I want so badly to live sometimes I forget
that I am alive. That this is enough—
even the fear, the regrets. That we have
each other, our children, this moment.
That everything

is a part:
even this difficult dance, the body getting smaller, thinner,
the lips getting chapped, dried out, the heart
getting ready to stop—

Put the music on.
Praise the sky and the stones that also
breathe into this moment, now:

and then, something else.

The End of History

History, I say, with its high ramparts, its engraved swords.

I say the bees are falling from the skies, the apples will not
    come into bloom this year

or next. The fish gorge themselves on plastic.

Or I say the sky is blue today with nimbus clouds.

I say the girl, her clothes ripped off, underneath the guard's
    heavy weight,

is named Deborah. I say the child frozen at his mother's breast
    has stopped

his cries. We must do something.

I say the hawk sits in the high branches.

I say the mother sits on the cold cement floor.

I say yesterday I was full of fear and today the sky is blue with
    nimbus clouds.

We must act quickly. The world loves itself,

falls into itself with open arms, devoured, devouring.

Adulthood

I want to translate
the spruce forest of my heart.

The animals are just waking up
but the snow has not yet melted

and the nights are still cold.

Speak, speak, I say,
afraid I'll never get home.

What happened in that childhood long ago?

I try to recognize me in my hands,
in my speech, in the smell of my body next to yours,

but everything is foreign.

                    Even today, in the light.

Outside, a garbage truck clangs and clutters
and comes to a stop.

It's Monday again.

Who is that under the branches,
crouching down among the needles?

What is it I am looking for?

4 a.m.

Outside, the streetlight is still on
     under the half May moon,

its marble face broken off
        as if it has been dropped.

     If I offer a poem to my loneliness,
     it goes something like this:

lonely the moon that orbits the earth
one side in shadow, one side lit—

     Just as in the monastery
     I was taught to say a poem

     when I wake up,
     when I put on my clothes,

     when I brush my teeth:
Brushing my teeth and rinsing my mouth,

I vow to speak purely and lovingly.
     And still my heart longs.

My husband in bed sleeping,
my children sleeping:

where will I meet
myself?

Will I recognize
the fullness,   all of us

cresting now into dawn?

Oh: let me accept
each day a small part

of this orbiting loneliness.

The Physical World

For nine months
I anticipated,

as the other end
of pain,

a revelation:
a world turned

inside out,
the sure logic

of arithmetic undone.
Each inch I grew

marked a failure
and a promise:

my present physical
certainty, my approaching

release. But instead,
torn open,

I gave birth
to the end of ideas.

Beyond pain was born
no understanding,

beyond understanding
was revealed

no new way of knowing,
new sight,

but another body,
robust

which no thought
set screaming,

purple-faced,
infuriated at air,

or moved closer
to my breast,

or closed its thinly lidded
round brown eyes,

so soon worn out
by the unfamiliar light.

Anxiety

I

I come back to the house, the children safe at daycare,
and the voice, leering, starts at it again: *If you would tell me*
once and for all to go away ... and while I'm still sitting
there, it drops that tone, and says: *Stupid!*
Come here; go back; stand up; sit down—the self
like some dog to follow the commands.
To do: call R; wash floor; take out meat
from freezer; draft letter to B.
I take the dinner, unwrap it. The styrofoam is frozen
on; when I try to pry it away, only a little piece breaks off;
I put the dinner on a plate as is, the rest stuck on; now pick up
the phone. When I tell R that her weekend score was—
not so good—I put on my sweetest voice. Take pail
and mop; run water. The water slops from the pail
to the floor. I push it around—underneath the stove.

But what if, when I walk into the house,
it happens differently? When the voice starts in that
    all-so-innocent
tone, I say okay and turn my back: here is the house
of my life, here are my hands, my arms.
If I think it, I can move my hands and arms;
I can move my feet and legs, the air around me moving out
to make room for me. Or I can choose to remain
perfectly still—

but it is happening again: Stop, I say.
I am in the middle of the room, not dancing,
not perfectly still, but carrying the milk back to the fridge.
Come here. This is actual. Stop, I say, why do you
say things not for me but against me? I choose not
to come, but to sit (for what is space
but a clock?) *If that is how you feel ...,* says the voice,
as if it didn't already know it. I stand. *Well, you have done very
    nicely,*
not even needing my commands. For mind, wandering out,
hits a body that must eat. Stop. For mind wandering out
hits the clock:

Or differently: come into the rest of the house.
Phone rings. No voice, or rather, out loud the voice
of someone I know telling me she has gotten sick
and cannot make it to lunch tomorrow. Hang up. Enter voice.
Write B, says the voice. Stop. See all this space around
me? No one is watching. *Write B,* says the voice,
now more urgent. No; my hands are my own.
For now—for how long?

I can do one of many
things. I can do two things, three things at once:
standing perfectly still, except for my hand, which now is
    moving,
except for my thought, which is moving my hand. *Write B.*
Someone is watching. But I have choice. *Because you know*
it matters that you not retreat into your life as a house,
that you remain in touch. Stop. *It is for your own good*
that I am speaking. That you rise up. Stop.
In the mind of B when you have written. Stop.
That you not disappear.

Or perhaps not the letter to be written
first, but the phone call to be made before the dinner is taken
from the freezer: that the fight with the voice have different
    (not the same)
outcomes, though it always gets its way: that the variations
are the play of me, this being done or not done
before this other thing, the whole of the game—
the delay before the accomplishment
that is no accomplishment, but another kind of delay—
(my hands, my arms) (me being in the middle of the clock)
(fighting voice). And the belief that for once, things may go
differently: me, not listening, in a perfect simplicity, being
    alone.

"You know," E tells me, repeatedly, "you shouldn't fight it
so hard. You are you if you are cooking, sitting,
talking in a windowless room. Order makes
no difference." And what if he is right? If
I could sit back and do
nothing. Or do everything exactly as I would like
to do.

II

eat & clean.
money & write.
in the closed box
of the three hours & a half
while the children
are attended,
let me grant,
for this space,
that nothing
is missing.
let the box
close on meaning;
everything meaning
itself, yet symmetric:
that to eat
is to eat is to
clean as is money
to write.
or that, if the voice
says differently,
to write is to write,
as to clean is to clean
as is money to eat.
see how perfectly—
and when i sit
down to write?

and i am still here:
look at the page
that is clean
and that means,
when i write,
nothing
that is missing.

III

What is missing? In the house of my life. In the moment of
my life. In the kitchen opening the refrigerator door
putting away the milk. When the voice comes. And I try to turn
    it off.
                                    In the house of my
life. Where doing nothing is sitting
down in the living room in the house of
my life on the couch. Where I have turned off
voice. Where in the moment for one minute
I am alone. With nothing. Doing nothing. No
voice. And what is there then? Not nothing.
But something creeping up. I say in the house
of my life. I say in the moment of my life in the
me. Which is something. If I sit perfectly still
on the couch I am me. So sitting still is something. And
    moving
also not a nothing into which I slip. For what is creeping
up.   For what is:

What We Are Taught

See all the children in the sandbox intent
at their work. It's a beautiful day. Perfect.
Strange in its clarity: not a cloud in the sky
and a sliver of moon still out like a mustache of milk.

At the edge, the mothers talk to keep busy:
what fine weather, one says, then repeats it
as the smallest boy puts a rock
in his mouth. *Elsewhere.*

Elsewhere—which is what? The town
in the desert gone up in smoke?
The body of the rebel soldier
left in the street to rot?

And they are all looking down
into the dirt-colored sand
to the red-faced girl with the shovel,
to the blue-coated boy grabbing it from her.

Or the wide savanna where the days go by
for the big footed cats, where the grasses
and the cats exist under sky, the same sky,
perhaps, not a cloud in it,

and the moon winks down
to a party of gazelle?
For night may never leave
entirely the realm of the senses—

"you must learn," they are repeating,
the good, the diligent mothers, "to share."
And the blue-coated boy now is red.
And the red-faced girl now is crying

because she wants it back,
what was not hers, that she might dig deeper
into the box she won't believe
has an end.

Memory

The self carries with it
a little self, and within that, smaller selves,
little boxes within boxes
of the self, and within that
the wild blossoms of the wild rose along the path to
the beach of your childhood, its tender scent:

Know, the body calls to itself,
what you know,
coaxing itself back,
not with threats now but with gladness,
making the space wide enough to want
to enter.

When your father said to you
that everything you did was
very, very good,
except for what was horrid,

did you believe him?
What was it that made you want
to abandon (oh, arms open,
splayed open) everything?

The self carries with it pockets
of sky, extravagant

at nightfall, a reminder of
what wants to
let go.

And the body, remembering
what it does not want to know,
nevertheless calls itself back,
away from the other voices,
to the little space, hardly a space at all,
the little hard nodule
of silence, that stone in the soil.

And the Small Body

The leaves rustle in the breeze as I prepare dinner;

>   the sunlight streams in, and I hear the blue jay's
>   rattling call

through the open window from the linden tree outside

  as my children do their homework

>   at the table.

And as I'm cutting carrots, the man comes again through the
  door:

>   and still my small body in bed sleeping:

in the other room, sitting silent, the oriental rug

where my sister and I play with dolls;

the piano I'll later practice; the long

>   bookshelves.

The past is the past

and the present the present except

for the ways it isn't. And I was safe

except for the ways I wasn't. And even into this
moment,

the ink spreads—

out from the very center of the dark, here,

into this kitchen,   this poem.

Catalog of Beautiful Girls

The girl with the open face feeding her sister from a bowl

of soup. The girl with braided hair skipping rocks

upon the water. The girl with her hand in her hand

listening quietly as the men talk, or the girl

at the window. The girl in the plaid skirt.

The girl who wears a string of beads at her neck.

The girl with the scar on her face. The one sitting, silent, in
the shade.

The one running down the street . . .

Stone Girl

with the stone face.

The stone throat. Stone hands. Stone feet.

See, in between, she is also stone and does not speak.

*

She is acting her part in the dialogue

like the wind listening

to wind. Or the wind

listening to stone.

*

Stone on wind. Wind on stone.

I think you are almost sisters. I think you have sat together a
    long

time. O: silence. What, from you, wants to emerge?

Sleeping Beauty

who receives
        the kiss—

Is this the story?

No:
Go back:
        After the party, after the celebrations,
        when the uninvited one sweeps in,

        after they told the girl
        not to hold the needle,
        after they locked
        the woman at the top of the house . . .

        there is still, always, the same middle:

No! No! I want to scream,
the instrument

                sharp.

And then, the bushes full of thorns,
growing fast,

and everyone
        sleeping.

Rage

Like all the stars,
like the dark that is again and again
pierced, like the silence that will not
close, like the flames that keep you
away with their heat, all you could not say
billowing in that conflagration—No:
like the flames that draw you in,
that open their mouths to lick, to bite,
to chew all the molecules and transform
matter itself into smoke, what can't be touched:

Knowing

The end (of what I know) occurs not at the end,
but at the edge of the middle of things.

Toys and plastic chairs lie scattered across the lawn,
the picnic table's spread under an arching beech,

but these human signs can't speak
of the necessary shift, and even the cloud

that cuts the monotonous sky with a brilliant pink
has nothing to do with this change.

The particular, the compelling object, breaks.
And alone, in place, remains

not the common master, waving long flamboyant arms,
but a self subtler and altogether more dangerous.

Out beyond courage and vanity,
I look back into myself:

like the silver-bowled lake
or the deep, impervious dark.

Reading to My Daughter

When you choose to read a book,
it's always a book about a girl.

I don't know if this means you have something
I have lost or if I have traveled beyond you.

When I look out into the world, or imagine myself
looking into the world, I see a window framing some trees.

Where are the people?

Who are the people of my world
that I imagine at night when I fall asleep?

But these nights I cannot sleep.

Imagine, I tell myself as I lie in bed,
a field. I imagine a field with a single tree.

But it becomes a burning tree,
its upheld limbs like a woman's.

What have I done?

The sky is the color of water.
The earth turns to stone.

I am thirsty. I want to drink.
I lie in bed looking up to the dark.

In the story, the princess
is about to take a bite from the apple. Know
I carry with me
a small stone.

I know what it is
to be touched

as a thing.
Small stone with no name,

I spit you out of my mouth
back into the ground.

My body is my
own body. I survive.

Know

I carry with me
a small stone.

I know what it is
to be touched

as a thing.
Small stone with no name,

I spit you out of my mouth
back into the ground.

My body is my
own body. I survive.

On My 43rd Birthday

Plato said the world was a cave, and we, trapped
     in it:
beyond the cave, the space of reality, freed
              from the illusion of the senses—

(Is longing the desire
to jump over our own shadows,
our own soft bodies, our own histories,
the man I did not ever want to know again entering the room?)

     What am I becoming?

Is it the December rain I'm
turning into, my breath the breath of Keats
and of the farmer in Nigeria walking down to the edge
of her disappearing lake?

The lake awaits the rain that does not come
     as I await an answer, crying out
in the middle of the night, looking
for truth, for beauty, for the understanding

     that will set it all straight.

And yet I know. What has been done:
What cannot be undone, even in its changing.

Summer Evening

The nightingale flies outside in the dusk,
singing and singing,

Philomela, with such sweetness, her tongue,
so that she stays silent,

cut out from her mouth. And still she
sings: *Too happy in thine*

happiness, Keats wrote to her
among the eglantine,

himself *half in love*
with easeful Death. No:

let me put the tongue
back in the throat.

Let me listen
to myself.

Hands

You who open for me each day,
who close upon a pen, a hairbrush,
a plum, a rock that I lift
from the shore and throw into the lake,

two in unison, in opposition, one that,
when the other is hurt, immediately helps;

hands, unprotected in the day—
dangling, un-shy, unselfconscious,
not full of doubt—
only yourselves.

Teach Me

how to pray anywhere.
Teach me that you live
not only in the open field,
the cardinals singing at first dawn,
but also in the concrete parking lot
of the Everett Mall, in the flashing lights of Old Navy,
in the wires crossing the open expanse
above me.

The cars speed down the highway.
Their tires spin, spin.
There is so much
work to do. Dark oil
flows over the whole land. Teach me
how to praise your whole body.

On the Shortest Day of the Year

Even if there is only the smallest door
made of stone,
with no handle,
bend low,
put all your weight into it:

it opens onto the wide expanse
of where you've never been—
groundless, blue, and untranslatable,

and there—just at the edge of your vision—
a single purple flower, rooting down.

March

All winter, we walked on the fallen sky,
walked on clouds until we fell, thigh deep, to earth.

Now the clouds are running down the side of the mountain
in small hidden rivers.

What in you needs melting?
What do you do with your anger and your hope?

All night, down the side of the mountain,
waters run together where we cannot see.

Underneath, the earth is awakening.
Once more the tips of bare branches

put out new buds. Again they clasp
their small palms together in prayer.

Imaginary World

The women who come to the playground;

the women who come to the market; to the bank—

for a long time, we lived in hiding.

Now there is no longer any silence that can break.

We've become supple

          like the wind, that holds nothing back.

My Throat

is a fire

is a line of birds
waiting to rise up from still water

is the earth
dark and heavy with spring rain

is the air
as the mist lifts, sighing,

                          ready to let go—

Outside the Sparrows Are Awake

and all the complications in my heart:

I, who did not know how to love

my own body, who mistook

the world for a task. Listen:

one voice and then another

amid the rustling of the leaves.

Happiness

I

Kingdoms for princes, souls
to guard over, large figures on paper
in the present day to ensure
that everything tangible one can articulate
can be procured (almost)—but without it,
every inheritance is small: the glass plate,
the polished doorknobs, the richly textured
Turkish carpets await a purpose.
It never arrives.

                    For each of us
thinks of happiness as something important
we would like to achieve.
And no one, not even the philosophers, can persuade us
we are wrong in our desire. Intent
on teaching, the thinkers never get it right:
not the indrawn eye to the body's amusements,
nor the call to duty,
nor the middle way (which is as close
as we have come) (in a world
where rules are easily disproved)
will allow for the sheer pleasure of waking
on a morning beside you, when suddenly
all seems right, like the line of light

that streams, at equinox, through the ancient
Mayan temples: what is outside
aligned with what's within.

II

But if another is responsible
for the self-assurance that brings
unreflective gladness, do we then condemn
the people who are early begrudged the gift
of love to a harrowing life of long searching
for what cannot be found?

Crying about the house at the end
of a curse, a fist, a cigarette butt, is she
what can be said
for the next generation?

Or if constant affection
shelters her days, is she freed
from the ravaging disasters
of loneliness, shame, rage?

III

For, does not direction depend
upon what has come before?
Confused, a pilot flies straight down to the sea,
thinking she is flying up.
Deep underwater, a diver

does not know which way to swim
toward the surface, as a person,
trapped in an avalanche,
digs in the wrong direction.

So how can we believe in the good,
trapped within the dark of an unimaginable life,
with no green in summer and no projected good?
Wouldn't the mind falter?
What makes us think that one direction
is not the same
as all the others?

IV

And yet, in either case, the child
of love or the child of pain (though
are we not all, in some measure, children
of both?) later,
unsolicited, unexplained,
sits in the shade and suddenly
admires the white
petals of the daisy or,
from the grayness of the day,
a red berry
encased by a single drop of rain
catches her attention
and becomes her own: a little gem
of certainty from which direction
itself can come.

V

For belief, then, happiness is necessary.
And for happiness, perhaps, belief.
And one day it announces itself simply as:
today even the clouds, holding off
at a respectable distance, know that
we appreciate their shade
but do not need it, and that
we have found belief
in the touch of a body
not our own. A single finger
undoes all uncertainty,
and the grasses sway
in applause.

And we see that what gave us
this first belief, this happiness—
the never-missed kiss of our parents
at bedtime, a touch of our lover's hand,
or the movement of the wind—in the end is not
of great significance,
for here we are! And the
pain, injustice,
destruction, does not go
away, but becomes only one direction
in a story where there need, in the
end, not be a point,
and we keep unraveling the spool,
moving, moving, all along.

6 p.m.

A lake flickers after snow,
      and I enter the refraction,

like playing the piano—
      fingers moving under hand

as if to get somewhere,
      the hour stretched with Chopin.

In children, too, it's habitual;
      a group mazes its way along the street

like an amoeba under a microscope,
      each small form a part pulling out.

But once when the day still held us
      to itself, there was a sudden turning towards—

as when in Wisconsin, from the back of the car,
      I first saw the man in the moon:

those craters, the eyes, the wide shadow at center,
      the mouth. It was so obvious!

Now I'm always trying to forget
      so it can come again

naturally, like the cat through the crack
in the window above the garage

or the apple blossoms that cover the ground
like newly fallen snow.

Invocation

Sleep, like a golden rain,
         fall through me.

Hard earth, that resists the shovel's metal blade,
                      yield.

Buried seed, grow plump, split,
push out your extravagant green tendril
                reaching for the sun—

When Death Comes

what will I want back? You in bed
close to me. I've been so hungry
with a hunger you have filled—

you feeding me like the ripe lychees
the birds gorged on that summer
in Costa Rica as we walked barefoot
with our children to the beach.

Red skins on the ground and the white, tender,
flesh-like fruit taken in the beaks of the big black birds with
     blue feathers
who dropped, when they were done, the smooth brown pits
of the fruit from the treetops—those birds
whose names we never learned.

Your abdomen, your thighs,
your chest, your fingers, your mouth
that I touch, touch me

          once and once and once

beyond all counting.

August

For six years, we took no precaution
and my body made no baby—
nor did we plot to create
another life, content
to let nature do what it would do,

which was, this morning,
bring bright red blood
in the toilet,
so bright and sudden
in its burst it seemed almost
alive, and then a little plop.

Child we will never have. End
of something.

In the course I'm taking, we are taught
happiness is found
in the deep I, in the consciousness
of consciousness.
But I resist.

I want blood and bone,
our son in my arms,
our daughter's laugh,
her wonder and unapologetic tears.

I want relationship,
the grass that grows no place
but the earth,
this earth, the stubbly
green beneath our bare
feet when we ran on the lawn,
the rich smell of dirt, the pebbles,
the grit, those summers when
we were all so much younger
and didn't know—such gifts!

As now, our children almost grown,
we hardly know this is as close
to heaven as we can come—

So close to so many changes, the ice
even now melting at the poles,

and see: these tiny red tomatoes at the ends of the plants,
little globes of sun, offerings
we pick and eat whole.

Arrival

Not, like Venus, come ashore
on a shell, but out of my own body,

you arrived. First one
and then the other.

Son, daughter,
as if time—those years

between your births—were folded
and the two births became

one double-emergence,
you, and you, and none other.

The clouds part,
and Helios rides the golden Sun,

glowing, across the sky again.
But not forever.

Counted are even the blades of grass,
the blades of wheat.

And among them, two,
born human: you!

And I, the carriage and horse
who brought you here—

the unextraordinary,
an unmemorable woman,

giving birth to this
wonder.

As if I were the chariot
of the whole world's becoming:

what happens
every day.

What is not infinite.
What does not stay.

Onion

wrapped in your own
paper-thin gold; your roots
shoot earthward; your top
stretches to the sun: bulb
full as birdsong.

Today Like Yesterday

and the day before: it's happening.

It's so simple, I hardly need any language.
Right there, through the window.

And in the trees, hardly visible, the birds
are back and going about their own business.

Do they remember their long journey?
The tall buildings, the wires?

Are they singing for the ones who are absent?
Are they, like me, singing to welcome in the dawn?

While everyone else in my family is sleeping,
the city is taken over by their song.

And everything, bathed in the silver light of morning,

is part of another story and its own.

Amid So Much Suffering,
Do I Dare Be Happy?

Every kiss that was ever kissed—
every smile, every baby's delight,
a first step, a face that hides
and comes back, a belly laugh—

every morning of gladness,
gladness, that selfsame word I
know because I've felt it—
every today, every yesterday

for a hundred years, a thousand,
ten thousand years
in languages now
no one speaks—

every grace—every kindness—
every head that bends down
close to another to listen—
every unchronicled act

of bodies helping bodies
so long gone we cannot
even begin to count
the occasions—

every one is framed
by great suffering,
by deceit, by threat,
by death.

No open plain
of justness
of rightness, no guarantee
of tomorrow.

But still, darling, your lips
upon my lips,
your hand on the small of my back,
my neck, my cheek—

just so—outside
of language, in every
language, across every inch
of time and space:

Joy, beauty, thanks
on the long path
through the meadows
where the forests burned,

through the grasslands,
the stands of evergreens,
the dark woods,
through cities, abandoned lots,

old minefields,
oil fields, we make
our journey; on and on we go,
again stumbling into love.

Midwinter

I think it's okay
to write another poem
about the light—about the white heron
who rises over the black oil spill
at the edge of the city.

I don't know if the heron
is full of joy
as she lifts her long torso up,
as she hurls herself (is that
what she does?) airward.

I don't know whether the heron
is going home or whether
she lives here,
whether she escapes
suffering or, more probably, not.

I do know there's no need to apologize
for my own gladness, today,
midwinter, that has no
apparent cause in the daylight cast
from the sun.

Power

I turn the questions over and over
when I cannot sleep,
when my mind will not turn off.

The waters of the ocean creep up the shore.
The temperature slides up
half a degree, then more.

The high glacial shelf in the arctic
breaks off.

What is it that I want?

At my daughter's camp,
at night when it's hot,
in the dark, the girls take off

their clothes at the docks
at the lip of the lake
for "special swimming."

I want to take off my clothes
for special writing
in a dark that is soft

in the water that will hold
me, my body still a girl's
with the whole world

before me, opening in song,
the words not yet written
on the page: O:

letter by letter, as the oil,
drop by drop, is coaxed
from the earth, is held

together, broken apart, taken
into the guts of fish, their
cells, our mouths, our milk—

Dare we ask for what we really want?

May I Greet You

as you might, in your best moments, greet yourself:

not fearful, not turning in judgment, not asking permission.

The gates are wide and many: look, here, this egg on the table

ready for breakfast, this tangerine, the winter sun

through the closed window: all are before you.

Taste. Remember.

And if you have no home to remember?

And no window to close? And if you are afraid

because the guns are not far, the fists,

may I extend a warmer welcome: may this page

also be your home, something to wrap around you.

And if there is no comfort,

let this be understanding. And if the end

is not what you wish and near,

let this be the light within you that has nothing to do

with outcomes. You:

beautiful as any flower, any agate—

Come: Touch the rough stone.

Rain Pours off the Eaves of the House

onto the concrete.
And finally, I open my throat:

world, I say,
of floods and droughts,

world of the red heart,
the heart of pink beneath the clouds,

of the tenderhearted, of the clenched-hearted,
of the troubled-, somersaulted-, suspended-hearted:

someone is coming to meet me.
The table is set.

And I am coming down the stairs to open the door,
dressed in blue jeans and a wool sweater with holes.

And I am knocking outside, standing on the stoop.
I think I am ready

to open my arms
right here in my own house

to receive myself, to receive the sacred
of this particular human form

on this wet day in November, the last of the leaves
ready to drop—rust, blood, brown.

12 a.m.

Tomorrow, all the trees will be bathed in white,
and I cannot sleep.

Beside me, my husband sleeps
so close, while my children sleep in their rooms.

All around me, in their large houses, my neighbors
make it through the night.

I: who wanted to chart my own course.
Tomorrow I will teach Hopkins.

I do not think I have ever seen anything more beautiful
than the bluebell I have been looking at, he writes, May 18, 1870,

> *I know the beauty of our Lord by it.*

The head is strongly drawn over backward and arched down . . .
> *the lines of the bell strike, rayed but not symmetrically,*

some lie parallel

As I lie in bed, my head drawn down, rayed with the ones I
    love,
with my own being, at this particular angle, I whisper to
    myself:

I am what I am; what Hopkins calls inscape

their inscape mixed of strength and grace

the clouds outside preparing,
and deep under the earth, the bluebells, too,

in their beds, taking just the time they need.

You

You, who were so quiet, didn't you know
there was a symphony inside you?
Didn't you know you were composing?
The trumpets are so glad
and the French horn, in its great deep beckoning,
resounds. Didn't you hear the calling
from your stillness, as if you had looked out
over calm waters to see the geese
rise up in unison in front of the setting sun?
Such a squall of color!
And your whole being given
to the one who rests in the great upflapping,
the geese mounting higher and higher

into the evening growing brighter and louder, still—

Postscript

Thank you for being here.

Writing these poems has been a journey to encounter the world and also myself more fully.

I wrote many of these poems when I woke with the dawn, or after meditating, when they would come quickly, as if they had been forming and were waiting for a release.

But in that self-encounter, I was never alone. To meet the self in the present, to go back and witness the self in the past, has been to encounter what is never solid, what is continually changing, what is always interrelated.

And in writing, I was in dialogue—with other books, with spirit, and with you, reader, even before I thought of bringing these poems together into a book, and with the whole world that is around us and that forms us.

In contemporary America, where so much is siloed and segregated, there is sometimes a misconception that this inner work of self-encounter is solitary, purely personal; but I believe that the inner leads us to the outer and the outer to the inner and then back out again.

To quote the visionary and revolutionary William Blake, it's our work and gift:

To see a World in a Grain of Sand
And a Heaven in a Wild Flower
Hold Infinity in the palm of your hand
And Eternity in an hour.

In encountering myself and coming to accept myself as I am, I also needed to encounter my past, which included violence and a violation that I did not, for a long time, want to admit. And in coming to accept myself as I am, I needed to accept the world as it is.

We find ourselves in a world of trance: we are surrounded by senseless destruction, injustice, inequity. To accept is not to condone or to become passive. Rather, to see the truth is to wake up.

In a time of unprecedented change, the very health of our ecosystem, the lungs and blood of this planet, are endangered. How do we address that?

The climate activist Gus Speth wrote, "I used to think the top global environmental problems were biodiversity loss, ecosystem collapse, and climate change. I thought that with thirty years of good science we could address these problems. But I was wrong. . . . We need a spiritual and cultural transformation—and we scientists don't know how to do that."

We need many forms of action—political, technological, educational, and also spiritual and emotional and artistic.

To see the world as it is can itself be a great act of courage and change. We see; we speak; we act—this often involves breaking silences on a number of levels.

Truth grounds us, and this truth encompasses not only the troubles of the world, but also the infinite forms of beauty, connection, and joy. After all, these are the qualities we're working toward, qualities that can only be found right here, on this earth; this is the only place we can hear birdsong, the only place we ourselves can sing.

My wish is that these poems invite greater awareness, expression, and engagement on every level. I believe we need many different kinds of action, and I hope this book helps build bridges.

These poems are for you. I hope you take them into your life and they become part of your own inner—and outer—dialogue and engagement.

Here we are at this moment. What do we want for the next? Where do we turn our eyes, our feet, our hearts, our mouths, our hands?

With love,
Nadia

P.S. To connect and to download resources for writers, activists, and more, visit nadiacolburn.com. I love to hear from you!

Acknowledgments

With appreciation to the editors at the following journals and anthologies, which published these poems, sometimes in earlier versions.

> *All We Can Hold: Poems of Motherhood* (Sage Hill Press): "What We Are Taught"
> *Appalachia:* "March"
> *Boston Review:* "The Physical World"
> *Canary (canarylitmag.org):* "Upflying"
> *Colorado Review:* "Anxiety," "Happiness"
> *The Curator:* "My Throat," "Today Like Yesterday," "When Death Comes"
> *EcoTheo Review:* "Midwinter"
> *Harvard Review:* "Smaller Even than Last Week"
> *Kestrel:* "On My 43rd Birthday"
> *The New Yorker:* "Knowing"
> *On Being* on their website, *onbeing.org*: "Teach Me"
> *On the Seawall:* "I Think It Is Such a Beautiful," "Arrival"
> *Pangyrus:* "Amid So Much Suffering, Do I Dare Be Happy?"
> *Salamander:* "The End of History"
> *Slate:* "6 p.m."

I want to thank the following readers, who helped with individual poems and with the whole manuscript. Always my first, last, and most trusted reader, Eric Colburn, and also much gratitude to each: Andrea Baker, Hadara Bar-Nadav, Carrie Bennett, Jennie Browne, Iris Dunkle, Jorie Graham, Kasey Jueds, Radha Marcum, and Sasha Steensen.

Eric, Gabriel, and Simone, you inspire me in so many ways. I am unbelievably lucky to get to love you, share my life with you, and learn from you. You light my way.

To Katia, my sister, I am grateful for your friendship, love, and support; and to my nephews, Declan, Nathan, Bowie, and Asher: it's a joy to be part of your lives. To my whole extended family and in-laws, endless thanks.

Thank you to Linda Camlin, Jayme Shorin, Cathy Conrade, Kim Cavins, and Kirstin Hotelling Zona for helping me get here.

Thank you, also, to Lisa Williams, Patrick O'Dowd, and the whole team at the University Press of Kentucky. It is an honor and pleasure to work with you.

Gratitude to the countless poets whose works have influenced and touched me.

And to you, my readers, my thanks. My hope is that this book touches you; it is written largely for you.